CHI DELISH.

No Experience Necessary

BROOKE ZIMMERMANN

Dedication

For my husband Daniel, and children Noah, Graham, Braxtyn, Cozette, and Quinn. Because you insisted on eating three (or 20) times a day, so began my love for long talks over chopping vegetables, life lessons in sink water, and theology around the dinner table.

Acknowledgments

Thank you to all the women in my life who made food, shared recipes, and broke bread and coffee beans in your kitchen with me. A special thanks to my mom for instilling the importance of pouring love into meals.

About the Author

Brooke Zimmermann is a wife, homeschool mom, home designer, and accidental chef. Cooking for her husband, five children, and all their friends has prompted Brooke to become a connoisseur of cheap, easy, delicious meals. Recognizing the need for young adults to navigate the kitchen confidently, she conceived the idea for "***Cheap.Easy.Delish.***" — a cookbook to empower them with the ability to make simple, homemade meal.

Table of Contents

SIMPLE MEALS AND EASY GROCERY LISTS

For The Newly Declared Adult

(who now must fend for themselves in the kitchen)

How to Use this Book:

Every recipe is simple, but some have an Easy-Peasy Version and an Intermediate Version. The Intermediate Version is usually a bit more homemade, but both versions taste great. When you decide on the meal you'll eat that day or to prep for the week, scan the QR code below, and you can access "how-to" videos and the food list for each recipe. For easy grocery shopping, screenshot the list! Follow the instructions, and you will almost feel like you're at home...especially since you have to do the dishes and take out the trash. Also, don't forget to buy the "green" stuff to make a side dish so that you grow big and strong!

Love, Mom

Chicken Soup with Doritos

Easy-Peasy:

1 rotisserie chicken, 2 cans cream of mushroom soup, 1 can green chilis, 1 packet taco seasoning, 1/2 jar picante salsa, 1 can diced tomatoes

Intermediate:

Substitute rotisserie chicken with raw chicken breast (cook chicken until white throughout and shred or cut up into small pieces)

*Do not use chicken nuggets for this recipe.

Instructions:

Use a large pot and add all the ingredients. Stir on medium/high heat for about 30 minutes, so that all the flavors blend together.

Serve with Doritos chips, sour cream, shredded cheese, and olives.

This feeds a crowd, so invite some people over and tell them to bring the Doritos and some avocados for garnish.

*Free-loaders do the dishes

Easy Potato Cheese Soup

Intermediate:

4 potatoes peeled and then cut into cubes, 1 can chicken broth, 1 can cheddar cheese soup, 1 soup can of milk, 1 package of cream cheese, salt and pepper, Italian seasoning, and shredded cheese for topping

Instructions:

Peel and cut potatoes, then put in a microwave-safe bowl with 1/2 cup of water and place in microwave for 5 minutes. Put the canned ingredients in a saucepan on low/medium heat, stirring often so it doesn't burn on the bottom. When the potatoes are done, add them to the saucepan. Bring pot to a simmer, stirring occasionally. Add seasonings to taste. Top with shredded cheese.

*Grab a warm blanket and binge-watch your favorite series.

Six Can Chicken Tortilla Soup

Easy-Peasy:

1 can whole kernel corn, 2 cans chicken broth, 1 can of chunk chicken or 2 cups shredded rotisserie chicken, 1 can black beans, 1 can Rotel (diced tomatoes and green chilis)

Instructions:

Pour everything into a saucepan and stir on medium heat until heated through.

Serve with tortilla chips, salsa, shredded cheese, and sour cream.

*If you can't make this recipe, call your mom. I can't make this any easier.

Easy Beef Stroganoff

Easy-Peasy:

1 bag egg noodles, 1 pint sour cream, 1 can roast beef, 1 can cream mushroom soup, 2 Tbsp Worcestershire, a dash garlic salt and pepper to taste

Instructions:

Boil the egg noodles in a large pot. In a separate pot, pour the remaining ingredients and heat until well blended. Egg noodles are done when they are easily cut with a fork. Drain noodles and top with mixture. Serve warm.

Serve with bagged salad or canned green beans.

*Don't hate on the canned roast beef. But if you can't get past it, use 1 lb of browned ground beef instead.

Italian Sausage or Meatball Subs

Easy-Peasy:

Bagged meatballs, spaghetti sauce, sub rolls

Instructions:

Heat meatballs per bag instructions. Slice open rolls, and heat spaghetti sauce in a pan.

Intermediate:

Italian sausages, sub rolls, spaghetti sauce, mozzarella cheese

Instructions:

Cook Italian sausages in a saucepan in about an inch of water until cooked through (be sure to add water as it runs out to prevent burning), about 15 minutes. Allow the outside to brown after the inside is cooked through. Place cooked sausages into sub rolls on a cookie sheet. Pour spaghetti sauce on sausage and rolls, then top with cheese. Place in an oven on broil for about 5 minutes. WATCH CLOSELY! They will burn quickly.

Serve with potato chips and a bagged salad or sliced cucumbers.

*Make the meatballs or sausages and sauce early in the week so you can add to a sub roll and heat up as a quick meal on the go!

Simple Baked Ziti

Easy Peasy:

1 bag Ziti noodles, 1 jar of your favorite spaghetti sauce, 1 bag of frozen meatballs, 1 bag (4 cups) of mozzarella shredded cheese, and a dash garlic salt and pepper

Instructions:

Boil the noodles in a large pot. On a baking sheet - bake the meatballs in the oven according to the directions on the meatball bag. Drain the water from the noodles and put the noodles in a 9 x 13 glass baking dish. Pour the sauce from the jar over the noodles. Take the meatballs out of the oven and cut them in half. Then, add the halved meatballs to the pan. Cover with mozzarella cheese. Place the pan in the oven for 15-20 minutes or until the cheese is melted and the sauce is bubbly.

Eat with bagged salad or canned green beans.

*Make this for a friend who is close to starving because no one got them this cookbook. It will last for a few days and makes great leftovers!

Sweetie's Chicken Enchiladas

Easy-Peazy:

Use Rotisserie Chicken

Intermediate:

Use cooked and shredded chicken breasts

Ingredients:

1 small can sliced black olives, 4 chicken breasts or 1 rotisserie chicken, 1/2 cup milk or 1/2 can of evaporated milk, 1 can cream of chicken soup, 1 can green chilis, 1/2 onion chopped, 3 cups of shredded cheese, 1 small package white corn tortillas.

Instructions:

Heat the oven to 375. Shred the rotisserie chicken or cook the chicken breast until tender and shred (I like to cook mine in the instant pot for 25 minutes or boil the chicken n water until cooked all the way through). Combine all the canned ingredients in a bowl with the chopped onion, add the shredded chicken, and mix together. Use a 9 x 13 baking dish and spray with cooking oil. Place a layer of corn tortillas on the bottom of the pan, then add a layer of your chicken mixture, cover with some of the cheese, and do the same thing one more time. You will have two full layers. Cover the dish with foil and bake for 20 minutes, then uncover it and bake until cheese is bubbly (about 15 minutes).

*Be a good student and read all the instructions before you begin.

Sausage, Rice, and Spinach

Easy-Peasy:

Aidell's spicy sausage, fresh baby spinach, 5-minute rice, 1 egg per person, olive oil, salt and pepper

Instructions:

Prepare rice in a small pot as directed on the box/bag. Slice sausages and place in a sauté pan with 1 tb olive oil and sauté until warmed, then add 2 cups of fresh spinach to the pan until wilted. Remove from heat. In a separate pan, cook the egg as desired.

Serve:

Place the rice on the plate, layer the sausage and spinach mixture, and top it off with the egg.

*This may be the healthiest recipe in the book, and it offers a great amount of protein and carb-loading as an addition to a workout, so make this more often and don't leave out the egg!

Grammy's Fettuccini Alfredo with Bacon

The Only Version:

1 small bag of bacon bits, 1 bag of fettuccine noodles, salt, 1 stick of butter, 1 package frozen spinach, 1 1/2 cup heavy cream (whipping cream), 1 egg, 2 cups parmesan cheese, pepper

Instructions:

Boil noodles until tender, drain, and set aside. In a small bowl, mix the egg with the cream and set aside. In a large sauté pan, melt the butter, add the spinach and bacon. Stir until blended together. Add cooked noodles to the spinach/bacon mix and toss. Add the egg and cream mixture and toss gently until well covered.

Add the parmesan and heat until melted. Serve with salad and garlic bread.

*WARNING – USE WITH CAUTION – This recipe is a game changer and may cause people to think you are a professional chef with mad kitchen skills. They may fall in love with you and/or show up for dinner every night.

Award Winning Chili

Easy-Peasy:

1 lb. ground beef, 1 medium onion, 1 Tbsp. chili powder, 1 tsp. ground cumin, 2 cans diced tomatoes, 1 can pinto beans, 1/2 cup picante salsa.

Toppings: Shredded cheese, sour cream, olives, crushed tortilla chips

Instructions:

Cook the ground beef in the pot, dice the onion, and put it into the pot with the ground beef.

Add all the ingredients into the pot, let simmer with the lid on for about 30 minutes.

Enjoy!

Serve in bowls with toppings.

Serve with green salad and those cornbread muffins they sell in the grocery store bakery. (A piece of sandwich bread works, too)

*That doesn't taste like chili, which is why it's a winner.

Jan's Hot Ham and Cheese Rolls

Requires planning ahead (the night before, set out the rolls in the fridge)

Easy-Peasy:

Rhodes frozen rolls, sliced deli ham, and sliced salami (do not think you're smart and substitute the meat - you'll be sad), white cheddar cheese, 1/2 stick of melted butter

Instructions:

Thaw rolls out in the fridge on a plate covered in Saran Wrap, overnight. Right before making the sandwiches, press out the roll, lay 1 slice of ham, 1 slice of salami, and one slice of cheese, and fold over to make a new larger roll. Brush with melted butter and place on a cookie sheet. Heat oven to 350.

Put in a preheated oven for 20-25 minutes until slightly browned.

Serve with ranch dressing or mustard and chips and raw veggies.

*Let them cool down before taking a bite - they're called Jan's Hot Rolls for a reason!

Any Meat Asian Stir Fry

Easy-Peasy:

Cooked and diced chicken breasts or sliced steak meat, frozen stir-fried medley, instant rice, soy sauce, and 2 eggs

Instructions:

Cook the sliced meat in a large saucepan in olive oil or cooking oil until cooked through. Make the rice according to the directions in a separate pot. Add the frozen veggies to the cooked meat and heat up until tender.

Add the rice to the veggies and meat and mix together. Add the egg on the top and cook until done. Add soy sauce to taste.

*Meat and rice amount varies depending on preference. How hungry are you?

Easy Fried Tacos

Easy-Peasy:

Bag of white corn tortillas, 1 lb raw ground beef, cooking oil (like corn or vegetable oil)

Instructions:

Heat about 1/2 cup oil in a sauté pan on the stove. Oil needs to be heated enough that a drop of water would sizzle. While oil is heating, spread a thin layer of raw meat with a butter knife onto 1/2 half of the corn tortilla (using about a tbs. of meat). Lay it gently with tongs into the pan and cook for a minute, then fold in half and cook until meat is cooked through. Remove cooked tacos, put them on a paper-towel-lined plate, and add cheese to the warm taco. Repeat until you have enough tacos.

Serve warm with dipping sauces - salsa mixed with sour cream and/or avocados mixed with sour cream.

*Warning - highly addictive! Serve with my easy guac recipe.

Famous West Coast Burgers

Easy-Peasy:

(1 lb ground beef will make 4 patties) 1 lb or 2 lbs ground beef (How many do you want to make?), mustard, hamburger buns, cheese slices, hamburger toppings of your choice

Instructions:

Make 4 round balls per 1 lb of ground beef and place them in a large sauté pan on the stove. Press them flat with a spatula and squirt a tsp. of mustard on each one with salt & pepper (Trust me on this one). Cook and then flip ard smash down and cook the other side until the burger is cooked all the way through. Top with a slice of cheese and put it on a plate with foil over it to keep warm and melt the cheese. Then, add butter to each bun and fry it in the burger oil until browned. Put the patties on each bun and top with your favorite toppings

Serve with oven fries or potato chips.

*Tastes like In & Out Burger!

Poor Man's Burrito Bowls

Easy-Peasy:

Instant rice, can of black beans, 1 can of pinto beans, salsa, shredded cheese, lettuce, olives, tortilla chips, and garlic salt (Optional: bell peppers and red onions)

Instructions:

Make rice in a saucepan. In a sauté pan, heat the beans and add garlic, salt, and pepper. (Optional - sauté the onions and bell peppers in olive oil until tender, then add the beans).

Layer everything in a bowl and top with tortilla chips.

*For the "poor" vegetarian in your life.

Best Ever Bean and Cheese Quesadillas

Easy-Peasy:

1 can of refried beans, shredded Mexican blend cheese, about 10 tortillas, spreadable butter

Instructions:

Heat the pan on the stove and spray with a light layer of oil butter the outside of a tortilla and spread a thin layer of beans on the inside. Place tortilla with the butter side down and add cheese to one half. Fold it over to make a quesadilla. Cook until the cheese is melted.

Pizza Quesadillas

Easy-Peasy:

1 package pepperoni, shredded mozzarella cheese, 1 can tomato sauce, oregano, about 10 tortillas, and spreadable butter

Instructions:

Heat the pan on the stove, butter the outside of a tortilla, and spread a thin layer of tomato sauce on the inside of the tortilla. Place tortilla with the butter side down and add cheese and pepperoni to one half. Fold it over to make a quesadilla. Cook until the cheese is melted.

*Pair this meal with a coke and movie, for a cheap date night. No tip required.

Easy Salsa

Easy-Peasy:

Fresh tomatoes, red onion, cilantro, lime and lemon, garlic salt, pepper, cumin, and sugar

Instructions:

Chop all ingredients and put them into a bowl. Squeeze the lime and lemon on top. 1 tsp. garlic salt, 1/2 tsp. pepper, 1/4 tsp. cumin, and 1/4 tsp. sugar. Mix and serve.

*This is easy Picco de gallo (salsa fresco). Even better on day 2!

Easy Guac Dip

Easy-Peasy:

4-6 avocados, garlic salt, sour cream.

Instructions:

Mix together for a dip for Fried Taco Recipe.

*I don't take "easy" lightly. This goes best with fried tacos!

Banana Muffins

Intermediate:

If your bananas are brown, this makes them awesome!

Dry Ingredients:

1-1/2 cup flour, 1 1/2 tsp. baking powder, 1 1/2 tsp baking soda, and 1/2 tsp cinnamon

Wet Ingredients:

1-egg, 1 cup mashed bananas (about 3 brown bananas), 3/4 cup sugar, 1/2 cup oil (like canola or vegetable), 1 tsp shredded lemon peel (this is the secret ingredient)

Instructions:

Heat the oven to 350. Put muffin cups in a 12-cup muffin pan. Combine all the dry ingredients in a bowl and set aside. Combine all the wet ingredients in a bowl and mix vigorously or use a hand mixer – then blend the two together (gently with a spatula). Take a scoop of the mixture (about 1/4 of a cup) and put in the muffin tin - sprinkle the raw sugar on top (This is the second secret ingredient) and bake for 20-25 minutes.

*Store in an airtight bag for up to 5 days – who are we kidding? You will probably eat them all today.

Deep "Air Fried" Oreos

Easy-Peasy:

Crescent rolls and Oreo cookies.

Instructions:

Open the crescents and wrap the Oreo cookies with the dough, making sure there are no air bubbles and it's completely covering the Oreo. Then, place in the air fryer until the tops are browned. Finish by sprinkling with powdered sugar or dipping them into a cold glass of milk!

*No need for a trip to the fair!

Ice Cream Cookies

Easy-Peasy:

Pre-made cookies of your choice, vanilla ice cream, and colorful sprinkles

Instructions:

Make ice cream sandwiches and roll the outsides of the sandwiches in sprinkles.

*For best results, use Mom's Best Chocolate Chip Cookie Recipe.

Mom's Best Chocolate Chip Cookies

Intermediate:

Set the oven to bake at 350 degrees. Line a baking sheet with parchment paper or spray with cooking spray

Dry Ingredients:

2-1/2 cups all-purpose-flour, 1 heaping tsp. baking soda, and 1/2 tsp. salt

Wet Ingredients:

8 tsp / 1 cup of butter-flavored Crisco, 3 tbs. of water, 2 cups packed brown sugar, 2 large eggs, 1 tsp. Vanilla, and 1 1/2 cup of dark chocolate or semi-sweet chocolate chips

Instructions:

Mix all the wet ingredients in a bowl with a hand mixer (or vigorously by hand) until creamy. Mix all the dry ingredients in a small bowl and blend all ingredients together until the flour mixture is incorporated. Add chocolate chips, place spoonfuls of dough onto the prepared cookie sheet, and place in the preheated oven for 10-12 minutes.

*The FDA does not condone eating raw cookie dough – but I haven't lost anyone yet. You're an adult now, the choice is yours.

The List of Pantry Essentials:

Olive Oil

Canola Oil

Garlic Salt

Salt & Pepper

Italian Seasoning

Butter

Ketchup

Mustard

Pickles

Shredded Cheese

Baking Powder

Baking Soda

All-Purpose Flour

Sugar

Cinnamon

The List of Basic Kitchen Essentials:

Air Fryer

Sauté Pan

Medium Saucepan With Lid

Cutting Board

Glass Measuring Cup (4 Cup Capacity) Measuring Spoons

Measuring Cups

Can Opener

Sharp Paring Knife

Baking Sheet

Baking Dish 9 x 13

Tongs